VIDEO
IDEAS

Senior editor Carrie Love
Senior art editor Fiona Macdonald
US Editor Elizabeth Searcy
US Senior editor Shannon Beatty
Editorial Allison Singer, Kathleen Teece,
Megan Weal, Amina Youssef
Design Rhea Gaughan, Ian Midson,
Bettina Myklebust Stovne, Ala Uddin
Photographer Lol Johnson
Illustrator Molly Lattin
Proofreader Polly Goodman
Indexer Helen Peters
Jacket coordinator Francesca Young
Jacket designer Elle Ward
Managing editor Deborah Lock
Managing art editors Vicky Short,
Diane Peyton Jones
Pre-production producer Dragana Puvacic
Producer Isabell Schart
Art director Martin Wilson
Publisher Sarah Larter
Publishing director Sophie Mitchell
Design director Phil Ormerod

First American Edition, 2018
Published in the United States by DK Publishing
345 Hudson Street, New York, New York 10014

Copyright © 2018 Dorling Kindersley Limited
DK, a Division of Penguin Random House LLC
18 19 20 21 10 9 8 7 6 5 4 3 2 1
001–307953–Feb/2018

A catalog record for this book
is available from the Library of Congress.
ISBN 978-1-4654-6998-4

DK books are available at special discounts when purchased
in bulk for sales promotions, premiums, fund-raising, or
educational use. For details, contact: DK Publishing Special
Markets, 345 Hudson Street, New York, New York 10014
SpecialSales@dk.com

Printed in China

A WORLD OF IDEAS:
SEE ALL THERE IS TO KNOW

www.dk.com

Contents

⚠ Safety first

All the projects in this book should be done with care. Please be safe and sensible—especially when you're doing anything that might be dangerous (using electricity, sharp objects, anything sticky or hot, or doing stunts, for example).

Be careful and have fun.

Letter from the author

Creating moving images is a powerful and exciting way to express ourselves. We can share inspirational stories, real or imaginary, to help us understand one another, inspire, or entertain.

Be inventive, have fun, and don't worry if it doesn't all go exactly to plan. Allowing your original ideas to evolve throughout a project and not being afraid to experiment can lead to some unexpected surprises that can make your video even better. There is no right or wrong way to make a video, but there are things you can do to improve the results you get and make it a safe and enjoyable experience for everyone involved. Watch online tutorials for extra guidance and help.

This book is going to guide you through all the elements you need to get started and set you off on your video-making adventures.

Tim Grabham

Top
techniques

Knowing which techniques to use will help you create the best video you can. Discover the basics you need to know when creating your video, from using lighting to camera angles. There are many types of shot you can use to film an exciting video.

Find out the best way to use **indoor lighting** for your video on **pages 18-19**.

Learn which **types of shot** you can take when making a video on **pages 12-13**.

Discover the **essential equipment** and the **handy extras** that you'll need for filming on **pages 10-11**.

Follow the **video-making process** from start to finish with the steps listed on **pages 6-7**.

Discover how to use clever **moving camera shots** to create professional videos on **pages 14-15.**

Learn about the differences between using **natural and artificial lighting** on **page 18.**

Make your own **sound effects** and learn how to use a microphone on **pages 16-17.**

From directors to composers, and actors to screenwriters, learn **who is who** in the video world on **pages 8-9.**

Make your own **reflector** and gain key skills for using **outdoor lighting** on **pages 20-21.**

1 Brainstorm an idea. What story do you want to tell? What genre will it be?

2 Write a **script**, including the actors' dialogue and actions, and information about the scenes.

Take a video-making
journeY

Making a video can be as easy as using your phone to capture wherever you are, whenever you want. But for a quality video, you need to do a bit of planning and prep. This path shows the steps you could take on your video-making journey.

3 Choose a **team** to help you with the video. Who will do which job?

6 Pick a **location** to shoot, and decide what **lighting** and **sound** equipment to use.

4 Create a **storyboard** that shows all the different shots you need to take.

5 Write out a **shot list** to make sure you have everything you need on the day of the shoot.

9 Schedule a **rehearsal** so all the members of your team feel prepared for the shoot.

8 Make a **set**, and get together all the **props** you will need to tell your story.

10 **Shoot** your video! Make sure you get absolutely all the footage you'll need.

7 Prepare **costumes** and **accessories**, and help the actors plan their **hair** and **makeup**.

11 **Upload** your footage to a computer if you plan to make your video using editing software.

12 **Edit** your video, adding **transitions** that move from one shot to the next.

Lights

Camera

Action!

13 Add **sound effects**, **graphics**, and **text**, including the opening titles and end credits.

16 **Share** your video with friends, or **upload** it to the Internet and share it with the world!

15 Make an **ident** that tells the world what kind of videos you are going to make.

14 When you're happy with the project, **export** your video into a movie file.

Who's on your team?

It can take more than one person to make a video. Everyone has an important part to play in the process. Knowing what each person's role involves will help you work together and achieve results as a team.

Role call

Being the director doesn't mean being bossy. Treat each member of your crew with respect. The first step is learning what each person is responsible for.

Composer
A composer writes music for the video.

Sound mixer
The sound mixer records audio, checks sound levels, and sets up microphones.

Gofer
The gofer assists everyone on the shoot by running errands and giving a helping hand when needed.

Director
The director is the creative captain of the project. He or she guides, motivates, and brings out the best in the crew.

Producer
The producer keeps the project moving, from planning the shoots to making sure everyone knows where to be and when.

Cameraperson
The cameraperson sets up and operates the lights and cameras, often with a team of people.

Screenwriter
The screenwriter writes the story and dialogue.

Choreographer
This person gets everybody moving to the same rhythm.

Actor
The actors perform in the video. They may portray characters or perform as themselves.

Hair and makeup
A hair-and-makeup person prepares the performers or actors to look the part.

Stylist
The stylist works closely with hair and makeup, but he or she concentrates on the costumes and accessories.

Set Designer
The set designer is responsible for designing and creating the sets for the video.

Editor
When everything is filmed, the editor cuts the footage together into a final product.

Calling the shots

As director, it's your job to give people directions to follow. Here are the key words and phrases to use and the order in which they should be said.

1. When filming is ready to begin, prepare everyone by calling, **"Quiet, please."**

2. Let people settle. When everyone is quiet, call, **"Sound."**

This lets the sound mixer know to start recording and to reply to you by saying, **"Rolling."**

3. You then say, **"Camera"** for the cameraperson to start filming.

They will shout back, **"Rolling."**

4. Then, if you're using music, say, **"Cue music,"** and wait for confirmation that it's ready

5. Finally, you call, **"Action,"** and let the filming begin.

6. When you reach the end of filming, wait a few extra seconds and then call, **"Cut."**

7. If everything went well, move on by saying, **"Next scene."**

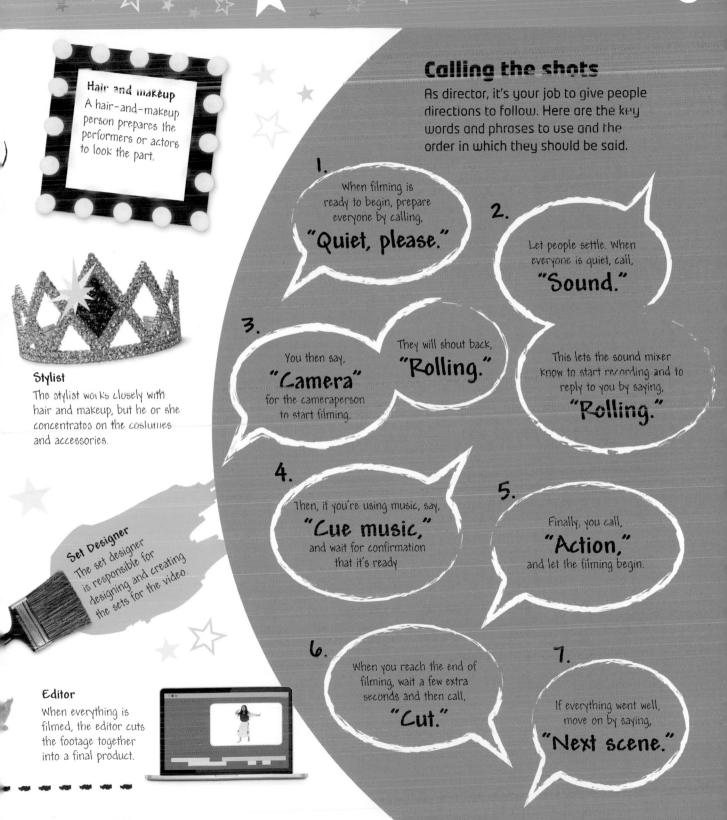

Collect your
stuff

It has never been easier to get a hold of the tools you need to make videos. You can use a camera on its own or with useful extras, such as a tripod, a microphone, or props. Your imagination and a bit of planning are essential, too!

Effects
If your camera has effects, try changing the colors in a video.

Lighting
Your camera may have a tool to brighten up a dark shot. If it doesn't, you may need to use extra lighting.

Camera
Choose the camera that is right for your project. Smartphones usually have built-in cameras, but you could use a video camera if you have one.

Focus
The focus determines whether the video is sharp or fuzzy. Most cameras can be set to autofocus.

Zoom
You can use this feature to zoom in on objects from a distance.

Other equipment

Some people use only a camera to film their masterpieces. But there are extra items that can make it easier to create your video.

Microphone
You can plug microphones into some cameras to improve the sound (pages 16–17).

Computer
You can upload videos onto a computer and make changes using editing apps.

Selfie stick
These make it easier to film yourself when you're out on an adventure.

Tripod
A tripod holds a camera steady. You could use it to create a time-lapse video (pages 58–59) where the world around you appears to move faster.

Props

Things that appear in the video are called props. You can make what you're filming more exciting with items such as water guns.

Types of
shot

Zoom in, zoom out! A shot is what the camera captures when you are filming. By coming in close or moving farther back from a scene, person, or object, you can create different types of shot. A variety of shots makes a video interesting.

Wide shot

Also called a **long shot** or an **establishing shot**, a **wide shot** introduces a location or subject. It's often the first shot in a video, unless an extreme wide shot is being used.

Extreme wide shot

An **extreme wide shot** shows all of the scene. In this skate park video, the entire park needs to be seen, as well as the ground and sky.

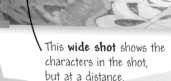

This **wide shot** shows the characters in the shot, but at a distance.

Mid-shot

A **mid-shot** is closer than a wide shot. Also called a medium shot, it's often used to focus on the dialogue between characters, show their gestures, and highlight their expressions.

A **mid-shot** focuses on the upper half of a person's body.

This **close-up** shows off the person's skateboard.

Close-up shot

A **close-up shot** frames a small part of a character, such as his or her face, hands, or feet. It can show a character's emotions, but it's also used to film **objects** close-up.

Extreme close-up

An **extreme close-up shot** focuses on a certain detail, such as a person's eyes. It lets the viewer understand what the character is feeling.

Moving
camera shots

Using different moving camera shots in your video will give it an energetic feel. Moving camera shots help you tell your story, because they reveal details to your viewers and make the action more exciting to watch. Here are four common moving camera shots.

STAR TIPS

- A tilt or pan can be done at any speed, but the faster the camera moves, the less detail you'll see. Try out different speeds to find out what works best.

- Try zooming out slowly to surprise your viewers by revealing something or someone that wasn't in the original close-up.

Tilting

Moving the camera up or down is called a tilt. Tilting can help introduce an actor, for example, by angling the camera from their feet up to their head.

Panning

A pan is when the camera moves horizontally left or right. Use panning to present an amazing location or to reveal and introduce the actors in a scene.

Pan the camera from one side to the other to show off a wide scene.

Tilt the camera upward to reveal the leaves and sky, or downward to reveal the tree's base.

Pan left to reveal the sea, or pan right to reveal the cliffs.

Zooming

Zooming in is when the shot moves from a wide view to a close-up in one continuous shot. This works well for picking out a detail in the scene, like a bird's face. Zooming out is moving from a close-up to a wide shot.

Zoom in on the bird's face to slowly reveal details—such as his playful smile!

Tracking

When the camera moves alongside something in motion, such as a bicyclist, it is called tracking. Keep your subject in the middle of the frame to make it seem as though the world is whizzing past.

As you are tracking the bicyclist, the rest of the scene speeds by.

Getting the best
sound

The sound in your video is as important as the picture. For example, when you're filming an interview or a show-and-tell presentation, the sound quality can make a big difference. Follow these tips to make your recordings really clear.

STAR TIPS

- For certain projects you need to record sound separately from the image. When they are combined in the edit stage, it's called "syncing" (pages 68–69).

- Use a clapboard or clap your hands to help with syncing. When you edit, you can match the clap sound on the audio with the image of the hands clapping or of the board being shut.

Using microphones

Most cameras have a built-in microphone, a device inside the camera that records sound. However, an external mic can be used to obtain an even better quality recording.

Use a selfie stick to avoid placing your finger over the mic.

Remember to speak clearly.

Built-in microphone
Cell phones have built-in microphones that pick up sound through a speaker. Make sure your finger isn't covering the speaker.

Keep mics out of the shot, unless they're supposed to be there.

Place a mic on a solid surface or in a stand. This will stop noises caused by a mic being touched or moved.

External microphone
If your camera has an input hole, an external microphone can be plugged in. This allows you to get much better quality recordings.

Wind protector

H wind protector is a fluffy piece of material or a soft cover that slips over a mic. It muffles any unwanted noise from the wind.

Alternative

If you don't have a professional wind protector, you can make your own by covering the microphone with an old sock.

Sound effects

If you want to add something special to your audio, use everyday objects to create special effects. Here is a range of ideas that you can try out, or you can come up with your own.

Crackle!

Thunder
Bend or shake a large sheet of aluminum foil.

Boom!

Fire crackling
Crunch up wax paper.

Rain
Sprinkle rice or seeds onto a metal sheet.

Drip drop!

Squish! Squelch!

Icky slime
Squish wet pasta in your hands.

Clip! **Clop!**

Horse hooves
Beat hollowed-out coconut shells on a hard surface or gravel.

Lighting for **indoors**

Pro: Can add atmosphere to a scene.

Con: The light will keep changing and the overall effect will not be very bright.

Disco ball

Filming indoors with artificial light gives you the chance to try out creative lighting effects. Before you start using lighting indoors, there are good points (pros) and bad points (cons) you need to know to avoid getting strange colors and results.

Pro: Fills a room with good, strong, overall light.

Con: Everything is lit the same, so it can have a flattening effect.

Natural and artificial light

When you film in a room where sunlight is coming through a window, you are using natural light. When you use lamps and other electric lights, you are filming in artificial light. There are a variety of artificial lights.

If you are filming in artificial light, your videos will have an orange tint to them.

Videos that are filmed with natural light will be bluer in appearance.

Camera settings

In your camera, you can set the "white balance" to make your picture cooler (more blue) or warmer (more red). Sometimes your camera does this automatically, but explore the options on your camera to learn to control the picture color.

Auto
In this mode, the camera will choose the best settings for the light.

Tungsten
When you are indoors using artificial light, this is the best setting to use.

Daylight
This setting is perfect for outdoors on a sunny day.

Cloudy
If it's cloudy, this will warm the picture up so it's not too blue.

Pro: Gives a pretty, sparkling light.

Con: Doesn't give off a lot of light so would not be good to light a subject.

Pro: Good, strong light that is ideal for lighting people.

Con: Can be unflattering if positioned too close to the set.

Spotlight

String lights

Shining a lamp at the ceiling produces a nice soft light but could create unwanted shadows under a person's eyes and chin.

Table lamp

Overhead light

Pro: Lamps with movable heads let you direct the light toward you.

Flashlight

Pro: Good if you want to create interesting, creative lighting.

Con: Can give a harsh effect when directed onto the subject or actor's face.

Con: Might be too small to give a good overall light.

Electric candles

Pro: Give a soft, glowy light to a video.

Con: The light will not be strong enough to light an entire set or subject.

Lighting for outdoors

Learn how to bounce light like a pro! The sun provides natural light, but the amount of sunlight can change the lighting effect. Take control with a light reflector to fix lighting problems and make a better video.

Bright and sunny day

Strong sunlight makes some colors bright, while casting shadows that make other colors darker.

If one side of a person is facing the sun, a dark shadow will fall on the side of their face that's turned away from the sunlight.

Ask someone to hold a light reflector, so it picks up the sunlight and bounces it back onto the person's face.

Cloudy day

On a cloudy day, the sunlight is blocked, so the natural light is soft. This makes colors less strong.

A person's face can look dull or dark on a cloudy day.

Colors, like the blue of this boy's hoodie, show up well with light bounced onto them.

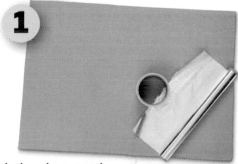

Ask someone to hold a reflector so it reflects the natural light onto the person.

The extra light gives the person's face a soft glow.

Make a light reflector

A reflector is a surface that bounces light. It can be made from different materials. Follow these steps to make a silver one.

1

Gather the materials

You will need: **cardboard**, **duct tape**, and **aluminum foil**. Cut the cardboard to the right size, about 24 in x 16 in (60 cm x 40 cm).

2

Cover with aluminum foil and tape in place

Aluminum foil has two types of surface. Use the super-shiny foil to cover one side and the less shiny foil to cover the other side.

3

Ready to use

Experiment with your reflector to see the effects of bouncing light in different directions and using the different sides. Try it with indoor and outdoor lighting.

Getting
prepared

What is it you want to show in your video?
You'll need to make a plan and get everything together before you start filming. Give it some thought: What story will you tell? What will your actors wear? This chapter covers what you need to do to get ready for your shoot.

Practice making your video at a **rehearsal** on **pages 34–35**.

Find out what you should bring to a shoot on **pages 32–33**.

Discover the different **genres** on **pages 24–25**.

Brainstorming

Before you get going, give some thought to what sort of video you want to make, and write your ideas down. This type of planning is known as brainstorming.

How long will your video be?

What will your video be about?

Will there be a story? If so, what should happen at the beginning, middle, and end?

Who will be the people or characters in your video?

Create a **storyboard** to help you plan your video. See the example on **pages 30–31**.

TITLE: "A Special Day" Scene

Notes: shot

Make your own **costumes** and **accessories**. See the ideas on **pages 36-37**

Think about the best **location** for your video. Read through **pages 28-29** for inspiration.

Learn how to write a **script** on **pages 26-27**.

Make a **shot list** like the one on **pages 32-33**.

Good **hair** and **makeup** are key to creating a style for each character. Take a look at **pages 38-39** for ideas.

Project .... Music video
Song .... "A Special Day"

SHOT LIST Director ... Sarah ...						Done
Shot number	Brief description of shot	Location	Actors	Props		
						☑
1	Extreme wide shot of playground	Playground	Paula			☑
2	Wide shot with lead singer	Playground	Glenn	Guitar		☑
3	Close-up of guitar	Playground	Paula, Matt			☐
4	Pan from left to right	Playground	Paula			☐
5	Mid-shot of lead singer on slide	Playground	Matt, Paula, Glenn	Balloon		
6	Costume and location change	In a sunny field				

Scene

Notes:

Mystery
This genre is about solving a problem or crime, often with a detective's help.

Historical
A story that is set in the past is historical.

Adventure
Exotic locations and action-packed scenes are the main elements of the adventure genre.

Choosing a
genre

What type of video do you want to make? There are many types, or genres, to choose from. Here is a selection to think about. To make it easier to decide on one, consider who will be watching your video and what they will find entertaining.

Musical
This genre combines acting with song and dance.

Which genre should I choose?

When choosing a genre, think about what works for you and your audience, or be inspired by watching films, videos, and reading books. Video makers sometimes mix genres to create imaginative stories, such as a historical sci-fi cooking show!

"GASP!"

Silent film
Instead of spoken words, a silent film uses music, mime, and title cards.

Action
This high-energy, fast-paced genre often includes a hero who saves the day.

Animation
The use of drawings, graphics, or models is how animations are made.

How-to
This genre shows how something is made, using a step-by-step technique.

Comedy
Designed to make the audience laugh, comedies are a popular genre.

Sci-fi
Aliens, futuristic robots, and time travel are usually seen in sci-fi videos.

Horror
Many people enjoy being scared by horror stories. Often this is done by showing ghosts and other frightening creatures.

Documentary
This genre educates audiences by documenting aspects of real life, such as nature.

CHECKLIST

✓ Make sure you think about the age of your audience. A child, a teenager, and an adult will all enjoy watching different things.

✓ Try to figure out what your audience will find entertaining so your video is interesting for them to watch.

✓ Don't forget to think about your own hobbies and the type of video that would suit you best.

Writing a sCript

Everything you want to be said and done in your video can be written in a script. A script acts as a step-by-step guide to what you plan to happen when you start filming. Writing a script can help your ideas come to life.

Characters
Fantastic characters are key to making your video a success. They are one of the most important parts of a script.

Coming up with an idea
Begin by picturing the type of story you want to tell. Consider where it will be set and who will be in it. After you have decided on this, you can think about the dialogue and action. Each part of the script needs time and thought spent on it.

Setting
The script must always explain where the performance is taking place. The setting should suit the genre you have chosen for your video (pages 24–25).

Dialogue and action
The script is determined by what the characters say and do. Make the dialogue and action exciting to keep the audience interested.

STAR TIP

- The best way to test a script is to read it out loud. If the actors run out of breath or get confused, then the lines may need to be rewritten.

Pen to paper

Once you have all your ideas in place, it's time to start writing. In addition to characters, setting, dialogue, and action, you can also include extra information in your script about camera direction or prop use.

The title of the project goes at the top.

The setting, characters, and time of day are written at the top.

Make sure you number the scenes so it's easy to keep track of what you are filming.

DETECTIVE DRAMA
Scene 4   Exterior of an old building – Night

BETH SQUIBBLY and EDDIE JESSOP approach the secret laboratory where DR. LAUREN VON SNORIN has been conducting her evil experiments. Beth walks forward and looks up at the building.

The dialogue is the conversation between the characters.

BETH SQUIBBLY
This is it, Jessop. This is where she has been growing the giant cats.

EDDIE JESSOP
(angrily)
Yes, and using my research to do it!

Directions tell the actors what to do and how to perform their lines.

(BETH pulls out a key from her pocket)

BETH SQUIBBLY
It's time to bring this to an end once and for all.

EDDIE JESSOP
It should have ended long ago, Squibbly.

Choosing a location

Looking for an area to film is called "scouting." Visit a range of places before you choose one. You might even decide to film your video in several spots. Find a location that has patterns, reflections, and particular objects that look interesting on camera.

What should I look for?

Ask yourself these questions, and use the checklist to figure out the best place to shoot. Do you need an indoor or an outdoor space? Can it be used in all types of weather? What look are you going for? Here are several ideas to get you going.

Slide, swing, or jump to create motion.

Create a vacation diary
An amusement park is ideal for a video diary. Show lots of details, but avoid filming people close-up who you don't know.

Make a fun music video
A brightly colored playground is perfect for a cheerful music video or as a place to show your friends playing and having a picnic.

Capture natural beauty
Woods create a perfect atmosphere for a drama.

Document an urban area
Use painted walls or a mosaic backdrop to film a documentary or an interview.

Use natural light to your advantage.

Create your own dance club
If you don't have access to a hall, cover the walls in your bedroom with dark material, and hang up a few disco lights.

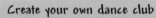

Make memories on sandy shores
A beach is an ideal location for a video showing a summer vacation. Capture details such as a sandcastle, rocks, and shells.

What is a
storyboard?

A storyboard is an illustrated plan that looks a bit like a comic strip.
It allows you to visualize your video from start to finish. Use it to make notes for everything you want to capture.

Drawing a storyboard

Always put the title at the top, write down which scene each shot is in, and add notes to each drawing. Your notes should describe the action, who will be in the shot, the costumes, special camera moves, any props, and the time of day it should be filmed. This example shows a storyboard for a music video.

Notes

- List camera moves in your notes to help improve the footage and make a scene look more fun.

- Keep track of what shots you have taken by marking them on the storyboard and shot list (pages 32–33) so you don't forget any.

- Think about performing the song a few times in different parts of the location so you can edit together a more visually exciting video.

TITLE: "A Special Day"
Scene 1: Shot 1
Notes: Extreme wide shot of playground

Scene 1: Shot 4
Notes: Pan from left to right on swings

Scene 2: Shot 2
Notes: Blow the lead singer's hair with a fan

For added impact, film close-ups of instruments, faces, or hands, especially if they are holding a prop.

Scene 1: Shot 3

Scene 1: Shot 2

Notes: Close-up of guitar

Wide shot with lead singer

Scene 1: Shot 5

Scene 2: Shot 1

For extra variety, add fun props or ask the performers to change clothes for different parts of the song.

Notes: Costume and location change for this scene

Notes: Mid-shot of lead singer climbing slide

If the video is for a band, film each person individually so everyone gets a chance to be featured in the video.

Scene 3: Shot 2

Scene 3: Shot 1

Notes: Zoom in closer on tambourine player

Notes: Back to playground, and add a tambourine

STAR TIPS

- While filming, you might get new ideas about how to put your shots together, so let your storyboard change if you want it to!

- Make your own storyboard template. Photocopy it or scan it, so you can use it over and over again.

What is a shot list?

Writing down all the shots you want in your video is a key part of the preparation process. This list is called a shot list. It will make everything run much smoother on the day of filming. This example shows a shot list for a music video.

Staying on track

Often you don't film each scene in the order it will appear in the video. That's why a shot list is important—it will help you keep track of what you've done and what's left to do.

Write what the camera will be doing, such as whether the shot will be moving (pages 14–15) or still (pages 12–13).

Scene 1:
Shot 3

Each box on the storyboard (pages 30–31) will have a row on the shot list.

What's on a shot list?

A shot list shows who is in a scene, what they are doing, where the location is, if there are any props involved, and what the camera is doing. It will inspire you to think about every shot and will help your shoot run smoothly.

SHOT LIST

Director ......Sarah......

Shot number	Brief description of shot	Location
1	Extreme wide shot of playground	Playground
2	Wide shot with lead singer	Playground
3	Close-up of guitar	Playground
4	Pan from left to right	Playground
5	Mid-shot of lead singer on slide	Playground
6	Costume and location change	In a sunny field

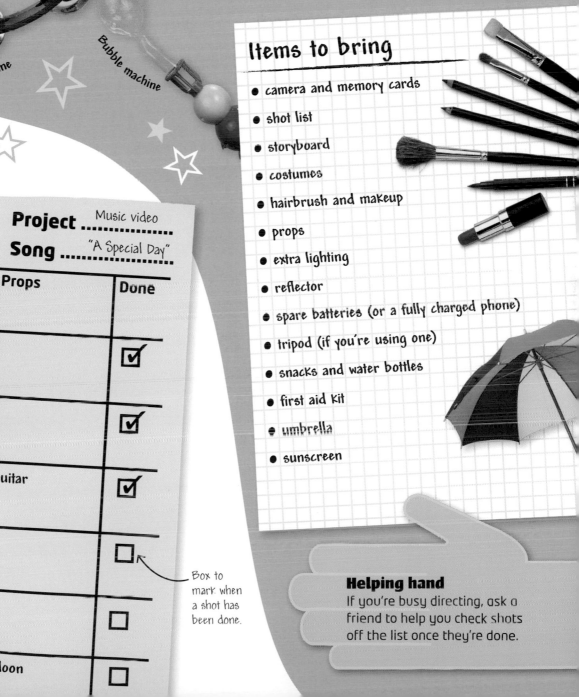

Tambourine

Bubble machine

What do I bring to a shoot?

A checklist of what to bring to the shoot is also a big help. It means that you can be sure you take everything you need to the location. It also allows you to check that you don't leave anything behind at the end.

Items to bring

- camera and memory cards
- shot list
- storyboard
- costumes
- hairbrush and makeup
- props
- extra lighting
- reflector
- spare batteries (or a fully charged phone)
- tripod (if you're using one)
- snacks and water bottles
- first aid kit
- umbrella
- sunscreen

Project .... Music video

Song .... "A Special Day"

Actors	Props	Done
		☑
Paula		☑
...lenn	Guitar	☑
...aula, Matt		☐
...ula		☐
...att, Paula, Glenn	Balloon	☐

Box to mark when a shot has been done.

Helping hand

If you're busy directing, ask a friend to help you check shots off the list once they're done.

What is a
rehearsal?

A rehearsal is a chance for the cast and crew to practice what they will be doing in the video. It might mean practicing the lines in the script or going through a dance routine. If there are props you need in the scene that have to be used at just the right moment, rehearsal is the time to try them out.

Practice makes perfect

Make the most of your rehearsal time by taking notes throughout and giving your cast and crew lots of feedback.

Before any rehearsal

- Make sure everyone is prepared, has looked at the script beforehand, and has learned their lines.

- Find out if it's possible to do the rehearsal at the location where you're going to shoot your video.

- Bring your phone to the rehearsal to film parts that you can play back to your actors when giving them feedback.

- Gather all the things you'll need for the rehearsal, including drinks and snacks for your cast, music if relevant, and any extra lighting.

- When the day of filming is close, run a dress rehearsal where everyone gets into costume, puts on their makeup, and uses their props.

In frame
If your actors are moving a lot, make sure you rehearse on camera to be certain the entire shot is in frame.

Boing!

Choreography
Make sure the dancers are in time with the music and that they know all their cues.

Costumes
Make sure everyone's costumes and accessories fit. Using these in rehearsals will allow you to check they'll look good on camera.

CHECKLIST

✓ Was anything missing?

✓ Did the script sound all right? Was it too long or not long enough?

✓ How did everyone work together?

✓ Was everyone in the right place at the right time?

✓ Will everything fit in the shot?

✓ Do you need to add any extra directions to the script?

✓ Did you give feedback and encouragement to your team? It's important to thank them and make suggestions for things to work on and improve.

Take a break
Give your team a break to get food and drinks so they're at their best in rehearsal.

Choosing your
CoStuMes

Most videos need costumes, whether they are fancy outfits for a period drama or simple T-shirts for a music video. The more effort you put into making your cast look right, the more believable your video will be. Costumes aren't just clothes—your characters can also have accessories, such as hats and jewelry.

You might be able to make a costume from things you already own.

Make your choice

Choose costumes that clearly show who your characters are. You could pick a big black hat for a pirate captain, a long white coat for a doctor, or a jeweled crown for a queen.

Make a plan

Do some research for your project by looking at pictures in magazines and books, or by searching for the topic online. When you see something you like, write it down or draw a sketch.

You can also collect ideas by cutting out pictures from newspapers or magazines.

Some costumes are easy to make yourself, such as this cardboard sword and shield.

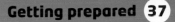

Should your character wear a hat? Some parts don't look right without one.

A mask can be used to hide a character's identity.

All kinds of different costumes can be bought online.

Some clothes and accessories can be bought cheaply from thrift stores.

Jewelry can help make a character look rich and important.

Don't forget to decide what the characters should wear on their feet.

Hairstyles and makeup

Hairstyles and makeup are all vital because they help set the scene. Audiences can tell a lot about characters from their looks and styles, from a ballerina's neat hair to a scary Halloween face. They all add to the fun of a video.

Using makeup

Always think about what suits a character. Do they need plain and simple makeup or a more bright and bold look? What hairstyle should they have? Do they need their nails painted, too?

Nails
Nail polish and nail art stickers add sparkle to a character's look.

Nail polish

Hair
Use hair elastics, color hairsprays, and hair pieces, such as feather clips.

Hair elastics

Feather clip

False eyelashes

Glitter

Eyes
Brighten up eyes with makeup, glitter, and false eyelashes.

Eye shadow

Face and mouth
Getting makeup right is a skill. You can look at online tutorials for help and suggestions for techniques.

Powder brush

Lipstick

Hairbrush

Face paint

Face-paint brush

Eye pencil

STAR TIPS

- Ask an adult to help you achieve tricky hairstyles or detailed makeup.

- Use makeup and face paints that are safe for people with allergies or sensitive skin.

- Actors may struggle to put on a costume after their hair or makeup has been done. Ask them to get dressed first.

Creating a look

Well-done face paint can completely transform a person into the character they're playing in a video. Cool looks like the ones below are easy to create through clever hairstyles, amazing face paints, and neat makeup.

Pretty princess
This character has an updo hairstyle complete with a sparkly tiara.

Dreaded Dracula
Ghostly white face paint and scary teeth help the actor really look the part.

Cute cat
Creative face paints and a kitten-ears headband set off this character's look.

Vicious villain
Green hairspray and face paint make this actor look scarily real.

Awesome ideas

There are countless video projects you can create. This chapter suggests ideas for you to try, from filming an "unboxing" toy review to making a funny pet video. Use these ideas (and more!) as a starting point for coming up with your own.

Make an out-of-this-world space **scene** over on **pages 44–45**. Then you can film in your own **universe**.

Present a **weather** forecast on **pages 46–47**, and learn how to work with an interactive **backdrop**.

Find out about the magic of **green screen** on **pages 48–49**. Watch out! Your toy **dinosaurs** will look scarily real!

I'm gonna be a star!

For advice on the best **setup** to show off your super **skills**, turn to **pages 42–43**.

Film a **stop-motion** race using toy **cars** on **pages 54-55**. Which car will win?

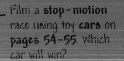

Learn all about **time-lapse** filming on **pages 58-59**. It will appear as if you've created **art** in minutes!

Play around with **scale** to make it look like a human is using ninja moves on a dinosaur on **pages 50-51**.

Uncover the dos and don'ts of using a **drone** on **pages 60-61** as you learn how to film from **above**.

Learn how to make the most of mistakes on **pages 62-63**. Don't worry—**bloopers** will lighten the mood!

Discover the best way to **"unbox"** a new toy or product on **pages 56-57**. Then make a **review** of all the best parts.

Let a funny **pet** be your guide on **pages 52-53** as you pick up skills for checking the **quality** of your video footage.

Show off your skills

Show and tell how to cook, bake, or make something amazing! A step-by-step video is a great way to share what you love to do and to inspire others to try it, too. Whether you're baking a cake or doing a science experiment, the trick is being well prepared and having the right setup.

STAR TIPS

- Clear away any clutter in the background so your viewers won't be distracted.

- Put up a "Do Not Disturb" or "Video in Progress" sign so you aren't interrupted while filming.

- Ask the presenter to speak clearly and slowly enough to be understood.

- Pause after the first scene, and check that the sound is being picked up.

Before the shoot

Preparation is the key to a successful video shoot. Before you can start filming, you need to think about exactly which shots you want to take. Have your storyboard nearby when you shoot so you can refer to it.

Setting up

Set up all of your props before you begin. Show them laid out at the beginning of the video. Make sure you check the lighting. Use any natural light in the room and bounce it off a reflector (page 21) if you need to.

Put smaller ingredients nearer to the camera so they can be seen.

To learn how to make a storyboard, turn to page 30.

Clear containers let your viewers see the contents.

Special shots

Using different kinds of shot will make your video more interesting and help your viewers understand what they need to do. Here are a few ideas. Turn to page 12 for more suggestions.

Close-up
A close-up shot like this will direct your viewers' attention to a specific action.

Extreme close-up
Zoom in even closer so your viewers can see the details of a technique, such as sifting flour.

Overhead
Shooting a step from above may be the clearest way to show what is being done.

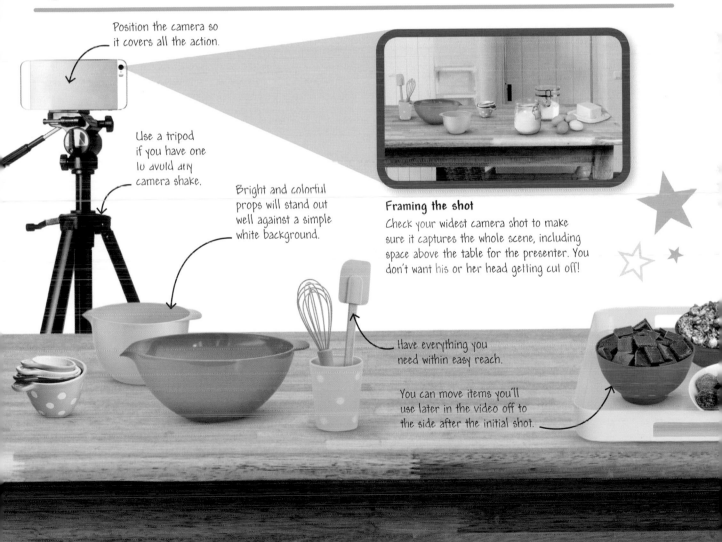

Position the camera so it covers all the action.

Use a tripod if you have one to avoid any camera shake.

Bright and colorful props will stand out well against a simple white background.

Framing the shot
Check your widest camera shot to make sure it captures the whole scene, including space above the table for the presenter. You don't want his or her head getting cut off!

Have everything you need within easy reach.

You can move items you'll use later in the video off to the side after the initial shot.

Shoot for the stars

Create a pretend world to set your video in. Make anything from an ocean scene to outer space. You just need clever ideas, recycled objects, and art materials. The possibilities are endless!

STAR TIPS

- Always think about how items will appear on camera.
- Add music to your video that fits with the subject matter.
- Ask an adult to help you with making a life-size set.

Make a rocket out of recycled items. Then use a dowel rod to fly the rocket in and out of your video.

Solar system set

Make your own universe out of recycled objects. Use glitter to decorate stars, tissue paper to make rocket flames, rubber bands to build a planet, and a paper plate for an alien spaceship!

Textures show up on screen, so make surfaces look real. Dangle items using string. Twist the string and let it spin as you film.

Create puppets to act in your video. Use bright and fun colors.

Other worlds

For a video animation you can create an entire set inside a cardboard box. Or you can make a life-size backdrop to act in front of by painting a wall or old bedsheet. Use cardboard, paints, and props to make your set believable.

Draw an ocean background, and make an octopus out of paper-mache.

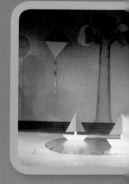

Build a life-size forest scene.

Use a dowel rod to suspend your alien spaceship in a scene.

Shiny surfaces will shimmer in the light, but make sure your face or the camera isn't reflected because it will ruin the illusion.

Build a planet out of rubber bands wrapped around each other in multiple layers.

Space travel

Use a transition (pages 70–71) to film a friend dressed as an astronaut in front of a space backdrop, followed by a close-up shot of a rocket flying. This shows the character is watching the rocket travel through space.

Use toys and small plants to create a desert scene in a shallow plant container.

Create a busy city out of cardboard tubes and boxes.

Forecast the
weather

An interactive backdrop is a background that is placed behind a person being filmed, such as a weather map or piece of artwork. You or the person you're filming can point to the backdrop and talk about the content. It's fun and easy to make. Grab your craft supplies and get creating!

Getting started

Use a large piece of cardboard to cut out the shape of an existing country or paint a make-believe map. Then draw your weather symbols and write the text for the forecast.

''Rain will be coming in from the East, along with a large number of tornados.''

Helping hand

A cue card is helpful because it allows the person being filmed to read the lines if he or she gets stuck.

If your cardboard is blue, it will be great for representing the sea.

For the land area, you can paint onto the blue cardboard or use separate green cardboard and stick it on top.

Add a little bit of adhesive to the back of each symbol so they stay in the right positions on the map.

You can make your weather report extra creative by including tornados, sea monsters, and UFOs.

Make a few copies of each symbol for when the weather is the same.

Finished product

Once your weather map is complete, use tape or tack (adhesive putty) to fasten it to a wall. Ask your presenter to use hand movements or a stick to point to the symbols. This makes the weather forecast more exciting and dynamic.

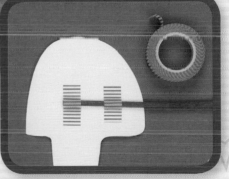

Tape some of the weather symbols to dowel rods. Then the presenter can move the symbols around so that they are not stuck in one place during the forecast

Go green screen crazy!

Green screen filming is an amazing way to create an epic video. It lets you put exciting, impossible backgrounds behind people or objects. You can try green screen filming on your kitchen table with a piece of green cardboard, a few lights, and models or toys—like dinosaurs.

How does it work?

Filming something in front of a bright green background lets you easily cut out the object and then replace the green area with any background you like.

2

Editing
Use the green screen tool in your software to remove the green background. Follow the instructions closely, or watch an online tutorial for extra tips.

1

Moving your dinosaur
Attach a strip of green cardboard to your dinosaur so you can move it around. The strip of cardboard can be cut out of the shot later.

Keep your hand out of the shot.

Use something heavy to help prop up the green cardboard.

Curve the cardboard so there are no folds.

Light the object and cardboard from a few directions to avoid any dark areas.

To avoid shadows, move the object away from the cardboard.

3

Adding in backgrounds
Choose a background to add behind your cutout. Your dinosaur could stand by a volcano or terrify a city!

Lots of combinations
Create fun videos by experimenting with ideas and adding different backgrounds.

Try sending your pet on a space adventure!

This pilot is flying without a plane.

Make your own monster

Play with camera angles to change how big people, pets, and props look in your video. Here, you'll see how to make it seem as though your prop is gigantic—or have the people shrunk?

How it works

By placing some people or objects closer to the camera, you can create the illusion that they are bigger than those that are farther away.

This line shows where the top of the frame will be.

Get down low and tilt your camera upward. The steadier your camera is, the better the effect will look.

Ask a friend to stand far in the background. They will look tiny next to the subject.

Place the subject near the camera, so that it fills about half of the frame.

Write a creative story about a monster dog.

Get creative!

Once you've mastered tricky camera angles, you can use them in all sorts of videos. Check out these awesome ideas. Can you come up with some new ones?

This toy dinosaur will stay put, but if you're using a pet as your subject, get ready to be patient. It may take time to get the shots you want.

Because the subject is near the camera, it looks bigger than the actor.

Ask your actor to pretend the subject is to their side, not in front of them.

Smooth ground, such as sand, snow, dirt, or freshly cut grass, will help with the illusion.

Try this technique for an action scene.

Add graphics (page 66) in postproduction.

Capture the perfect
pet video

Film pets on the go (pages 14-15).

Funny animal videos crack us up, but only when they're of good quality. You can't laugh at a dog playing the piano if the video is too dark or out of focus. To make the perfect pet video, you need two things: a hilarious subject and key technical skills.

Find fun camera shots (pages 12-13).

Find the funny

Animals can be funny creatures, whether they're chasing their tails or making silly sounds. Keep your eyes and ears open for video subjects, or help things along with funny situations, props, or costumes.

Planning ahead?
Unless your pet is really well trained, storyboarding isn't going to help much! Instead, observe your pet in advance. Then be patient and ready to capture the action when it happens.

Get the light right on an outdoor shoot (pages 20-21).

Light up funny indoor antics (pages 18-19).

Check for quality

Once you finish recording, play back the shot on your camera. It's good to check the first few shots in case you have forgotten to set up something correctly. Here are a few things that can result in a disappointing shot.

This shot is in frame, in focus, well exposed, and color balanced.

I look paw-fect!

Out of frame

If your subject is moving around a lot, it may disappear off the side of the shot. Hold the camera steady, and follow your subject as best you can.

Out of focus

The closer you are to a moving subject, the easier it is for the subject to go out of focus. It helps to stand back and zoom in instead.

Go glam with props and costumes (pages 36–37).

Overexposed

Underexposed

Bad exposure

The exposure is how much light is going into the camera. Try manually setting the exposure instead of setting it to "auto." It takes practice but offers more control.

Weird colors

On many cameras and devices, the color option is set to "auto." If the image is too blue or orange, you can change it manually by exploring the different color settings.

Set your props in
motion

Bring objects that normally wouldn't move on their own to life using stop-motion magic. Take a series of still images one after the other, changing the position of your objects slightly between each shot. When you import the images into your computer and play them all in a row, the objects will appear to move!

Find the best angles

Position the camera at dynamic angles around the set to make the video exciting. See pages 14–15 for camera angle ideas.

Ready, set, go!

Film a stop-motion race between two toy cars. First, draw and paint your own racetrack. Make the dotted lines down the middle of the track equal distances apart. Choose which car you want to win, and make that car advance three lines ahead for each shot. Move the losing car two lines ahead for each shot.

A little bit of tack (adhesive putty) will keep your car from rolling away.

Frame rate

A video's frame rate is the number of images that play for every one second of film. This shows a frame rate of 12, which is the most common frame rate for animation.

Imagine that

Stop-motion is perfect for making the impossible seem possible. With a bit of adhesive tack, for example, you could make your toy car race up a wall. Can you imagine other tricks you could make the car do?

STAR TIPS

● Stop-motion can take a while to film, but it's worth being patient because the results are magical.

● Turn off the autofocus and set the focus manually to help the camera focus before each shot.

● By varying the distance the car moves between frames, you can make it appear faster or slower.

● Lots of images are needed to make even four or five seconds of footage. Import all the images and choose the "12-frames-a-second" option in your software when creating your video clip.

Don't move your cars too much between shots, or the race will end too quickly.

One second of film

Think outside the box

What's in the box? Reveal and review exciting new items in an "unboxing" video. This type of video may seem simple enough at first, but if you really want to engage your viewers, there are some important things you need to know.

Clothing, jewelry, and makeup are fun items to show and review.

New tech products make for exciting unboxing subjects.

Pick your passion

You already know what subjects or items you're most passionate about. Choose your favorite topic, and go from there.

Tricks of the trade

All unboxing videos are different, depending on the subject and the reviewer's personality. There are a few tricks that most great ones share. Think of these steps as suggestions rather than rules.

Tell your audience what you are going to review. Make sure the shot is close enough to get a good view of it.

Demonstrate any features it has, and show it from all sides—including the inside, if that's important.

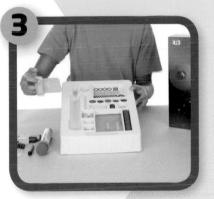

Show off all the pieces one by one. You might unbox the item on a table to keep any parts from getting lost.

Display everything clearly in front of you before moving on to assemble and review the product.

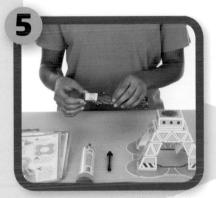

Explain each step if the item requires assembly, but don't let your review go on too long. Keep it short and fun.

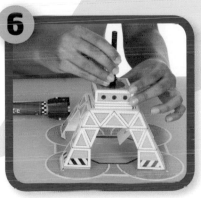

Use close-up shots to show off steps or items that are particularly tricky, detailed, or interesting.

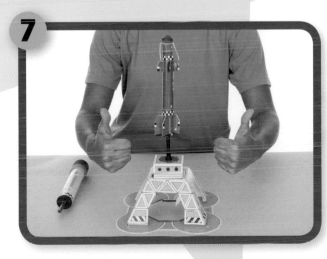

Say what you like or don't like about the product at the end of the video, and give viewers a good look at it. Don't forget to let your personality shine through!

Make a video using
time-lapse

Time-lapse videos create a sense of fantastic motion by speeding up the passing of time. It is a fun technique used to make events look like they're happening faster or for speeding up a long piece of footage to fit into a short amount of time.

Sunrises and sunsets are very popular subjects for time-lapse videos.

Film an art project

Set up your camera or your phone to record while you create a piece of art, such as a collage. When you are finished, you can speed up the footage using your editing software.

Film every step of the project if you want your viewers to be able to recreate it.

Before time-lapse: 20 minutes

After time-lapse: 20 seconds

Change the zoom or the position of the camera to get a different view of the action.

Time-lapse projects can take hours, even days, to film, but the finished video will be much shorter.

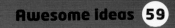

World of ideas

The possibilities for time-lapse are endless. Try filming clouds floating across the sky, a snail crawling up a wall, a flower opening before your eyes, or a cool science experiment.

Imagine how awesome footage of this melting ice pop would look sped up or played in reverse!

STAR TIPS

- Before you start filming, make sure there's plenty of space on your camera's memory card.

- Put your camera on a tripod or flat surface so it is steady throughout filming.

- If your camera can only record for limited periods, use this as a chance to change angles and then start recording again.

- Add some lively music to give your time-lapse video energy.

Make sure you get a nice shot of the finished work.

Drones come in many sizes. Start out with a small, lightweight one.

Shoot with a
drone

The camera sits on the underside of the drone. It films while the drone flies.

A drone is a flying machine that you can control with a remote. Some drones have cameras attached, allowing you to get overhead views that are difficult to capture any other way. Use a drone to shoot a whole video from above or for a few overhead shots for a bigger project.

Surf's up!

A beach is a great place to practice flying, as long as it is not crowded and flying drones is allowed. This drone shot for a surfing video establishes the scene and gives an idea of what action is to come.

Controlling the drone

A drone with a camera attached has four propellers that allow it to fly around. You can steer it with your phone while it films. The video will be recorded on a memory card in the drone or directly onto your phone.

View from above

Drones are ideal for filming big events, showing off scenery, or getting a unique angle on life. Filmmakers have found creative ways to use drones.

Fly high above a beach or park for a cool opening to your video.

This shot from above shows these surfers looking small next to the sea, setting the scene for an epic video.

✓ Do

- Do know the rules in your area so you can fly safely and legally. You'll need permission to fly a drone in some places, such as city centers.

- Do practice flying the drone before the day of the shoot.

- Do tell the actors whether you want them to look at the drone or pretend it isn't there.

- Once you get used to using a drone, do try out all of the different moves, and take lots of exciting shots.

✗ Don't

- Don't buy a drone without researching the different models first. Some may suit your needs better than others.

- Don't fly too close to the ground or to your actors' heads.

- Don't fly too close to animals. They may get scared (or your drone could become your dog's newest chew toy!).

- Don't fly a drone on a very windy day. This is dangerous, and it will be difficult to get a stable shot.

Use your drone to get a new angle on a sporting event.

Check out your local area from the sky.

It's all about the
bloopers

Many mistakes can happen when you are making a video. Actors forget their lines, props break, and sets fall down. Sometimes these problems are very funny! Funny video mistakes are known as bloopers. Many directors choose to include a short blooper section at the end of a film.

Your bloopers

When you start editing your video, create a new sequence and call it "Bloopers edit." Whenever you see a mistake or something unplanned, add it to your bloopers project.

OOPS!

Bloopers edit

Video edit

Video 1

Audio 1

Things to watch out for

All sorts of mistakes can be funny. Here are some things to look out for that could make good entries for your bloopers video.

Watch out for any pets stealing your prop!

Sometimes a joke or mistake can make the whole cast start laughing.

A slip or fall can add an unplanned funny moment to your video.

Your actors will have a lot of lines to remember. It can be funny if they forget them or get their words muddled.

Watch out for actors being silly—some props are too much fun not to play with!

SPLASH!

Editing and sharing

It's now time to add the finishing touches to your video, so it is ready to share with others. This is called the edit. You might want to add sound and graphics to your video or use special effects to make it look more professional. Just before you upload the video, create a trailer to get everyone excited about your masterpiece!

Turn to **page 69** to find out how to **sync music** to your videos.

Flip forward to **pages 72–73** to find out how to **export your video** into different-sized files you can share.

Starting your edit

Follow these simple steps when you edit. The better your selection of footage, the more enjoyable your video will be to watch.

Learn how to add **text and graphics** on **pages 66–67**.

1 Install editing software onto your device. Open it up, and import your footage into the "timeline," the creative area where you do your editing.

2 Put your footage in the correct order on the timeline. Cut down anything that is too long. If relevant, import sound files.

3 Play around with your timeline, adding text, graphics, transitions, or special effects. When you're happy with your video, export it.

Turn to **pages 70–71** to discover how to use **transitions** to move between scenes.

Make your own **video opener** on **pages 76–77**.

See how you can **upload and share your video** with all of your friends on **pages 74–75**.

Get advice on how to create an **awesome trailer** on **page 71**.

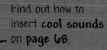

Next big thing

Find out how to insert **cool sounds** on **page 68**.

Adding text and graphics

Text and graphics can add information and style to your video. Text can be used for the opening titles, to explain a concept, and for the end credits. Graphics are images that can help present a statistic or make a video more exciting.

What is a font?

When you use a computer to create text, you need to choose a font. A font is the style of letter you use. There are many fonts to choose from.

Look through the different font options to find the one you like best for your video.

What are graphics?

Graphics are visual images. They can be used to represent something, such as a statistic or fact, or as decoration to make a video look good.

This graphic shows people's favorite type of pie.

A graphic as simple as a star can add visual interest to your video!

Start and end

Most videos use text for the opening titles and end credits. Like all other parts of video making, these need some creativity and imagination so they look interesting and match the theme of the video.

This is my Life

Make the **opening title** in a color and font that you like for the video.

A simple graphic can sit behind text as long as the words are still easy to read.

Crew
Director Tim
Editor Angela
Sound editor Jake

Cast
Old man Charlie
Hero Laila
Villain Joanne
Princess Alima

List everyone who helped with the video in the **end credits**.

You can check how the text looks in the **preview panel**.

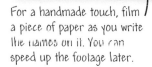

Starring:

For a handmade touch, film a piece of paper as you write the names on it. You can speed up the footage later.

The **tools** in your editing software will have options for size, color, and position of your graphics and text.

A great adventure

Drag the graphics or text onto your **timeline** where they are needed in the video.

How to do it

Type the text you'd like to use, or create or add a graphic. Then use the software's tools to adjust it until it looks the way you want. Finally, insert it at the appropriate place in the video.

Adding **sOUnd**

How your video sounds is just as critical as how your video looks. The sound doesn't need to be perfect when you film—you can add speech, effects, and music using your editing software. Thoughtfully adding audio to great footage can create a masterpiece.

STAR TIPS

- Make sure you have permission to use a piece of music. Most songs are protected by copyright.
- Use sound effects that come with your computer's software, or try making your own sounds (pages 16–17).

Editing process

Some things that go wrong during filming can be fixed as you edit, or put together, the footage. If the sound isn't loud enough or if you didn't say what you meant to say, you can add sound effects and voice-overs during editing.

Sound effects
Extra sounds can add drama to your video.

A suspenseful creak or loud slam adds excitement to a door opening or closing.

SLAM!

Voice-over
A voice-over is speech that explains what's going on in the footage. You can write this before you shoot so you know what you want to capture.

"After adding the eggs, stir until mixed..."

A voice-over explaining recipe instructions can be added to footage of baking.

Make sure you match up the voice-over with what's going on in the footage.

How to sync

"Syncing" footage to audio, such as for a music video, takes practice. You have to align footage that contains guide audio, which is music played on set to keep the musicians in time, with your master audio track. Repeat these steps for each piece of footage you want to add.

1 Import the master audio track into your editing software.

The master audio track is a file recorded separately from the video, such as a piece of music or a song.

2 Bring in the video footage, which has the guide audio.

The guide audio may not be quite as clear as the master.

3 Find a distinct sound in your guide audio, such as a drum beat. Then find the same beat in the master.

The drum sound is shown as a tall peak in the line.

Cut the footage where the drum is being hit.

Make sure the drum beats line up exactly.

Fun extras

Not all footage needs to be synced. Some clips, like these fireworks, can go anywhere you think they look right or respond well to the music.

4 Put your video footage above the master, and mute the guide audio. You're all synced up!

Transitioning
scenes

Transitions let you move from one shot to another in different ways. The transition you choose can suggest that time has passed, the location has changed, or an event is about to begin or end. In this way, transitions are powerful storytelling tools.

Types of transitions

There are many transitions you can use to change from one shot to the next. It's up to you to decide which feels right between scenes. Here are the four used most often.

Adding transitions

Deciding which transition works best between two shots can be tricky, but actually adding them to your project is easy. Follow these steps each time you want to add a transition.

1 Your editing software will have transitions ready for you to use. Find where they are, and choose one you like.

2 Select the shot that you want to add the transition to. If you're trying a cross-fade or wipe, select two shots next to each other.

3 Apply the transition to your shot, and press play to see what it looks like. Repeat these steps until you're happy with how the transition works.

Cross-fade

A cross-fade is when one shot appears on top of another to replace it. This transition helps suggest that a period of time has passed.

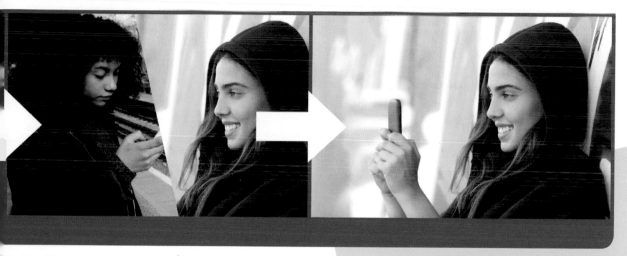

Wipe

There are lots of animated wipes, from straight lines to complex shapes. They "wipe" one shot out to reveal another. Look online for wipe examples to get inspiration.

Straight cut

A straight cut, the simplest transition, is when one shot ends and the next just starts.

Fade in or out

Fading in or out from black can be dramatic. It's often used to suggest something is starting or has come to an end.

Make a movie trailer

A trailer is a mini-advertisement for a movie, and making one is a great way to practice using transitions. Select some of the best shots from your movie, and then add transitions to make it exciting.

Exporting
your video

Exporting changes your video from the type of file your computer uses to a type of file that you can share. It takes only a few clicks, but there are some things you should keep in mind as you do it: What screen size will your video be watched on, and do you want it in high or low quality?

STAR TIPS

- Before you export your video, give it a final check to make sure you're happy with it.

- You could also get a friend to watch your video to make sure you haven't missed any errors.

How to export

Click "export" in your editing software to export your video. You will see various options when you click export. Here are some tips to help you as you make your choices.

When saving your video to your computer, give it the same name as the video title, and save it somewhere easy to find.

Think about what size screen you want to watch your video on, and choose a frame size to match.

If you have audio with your video, remember to export it along with the video, or you will end up with a silent movie.

If you want to share your video on the Internet, take a look at the recommended export settings of the website.

Frame size

The frame size tells you the width and height of your video, measured in "pixels." Choose a big frame size if you want to watch your video on a big screen or a small frame size for a small screen.

Picture quality

You can choose to export your video at low, medium, or high quality. The higher the quality you choose, the better the images will look. However, high-quality videos take longer for your computer to make and share.

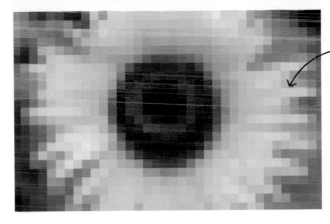

It can be hard to see what's happening on a very low quality video.

There are five different common frame sizes.

1920 pixels x 1080 pixels

1280 pixels x 720 pixels

854 pixels x 480 pixels

640 pixels x 360 pixels

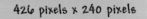

426 pixels x 240 pixels

Uploading and sharing

Once you have finished your video, you can share it with others. There are many places you can get your work seen, from local film festivals to school assemblies. Your biggest audience will be online, so you may want to upload your video to the Internet.

Going viral

If you upload your video to the right website, with the best settings, your video could travel around the world. Here's how just a few shares to start with can spiral into a viral success.

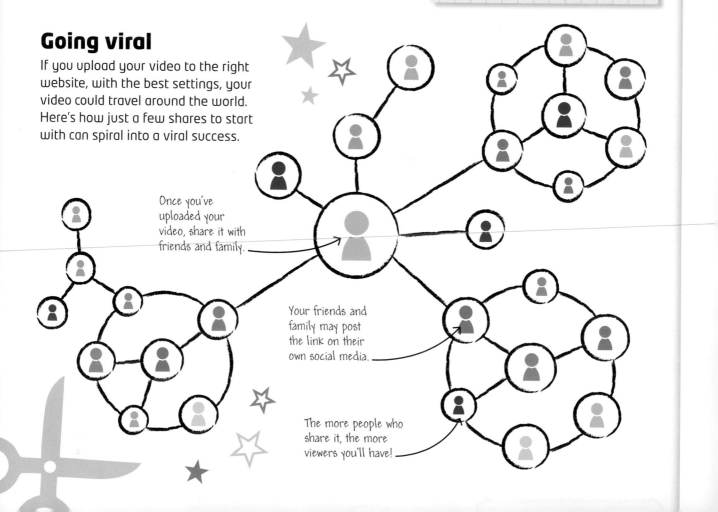

Once you've uploaded your video, share it with friends and family.

Your friends and family may post the link on their own social media.

The more people who share it, the more viewers you'll have!

Uploading your video

The most popular video-sharing websites are visited by millions of people—but they have to be able to find your video in order to watch it. The information you upload along with your video will help it be found

The **title** is the most important part! Make it clear and concise.

A short **description** will give people a quick idea of what your video is about.

My trip to the farm

I saw pigs and chickens when my family went to Freddie's Farm. Oink!

You'll likely see a small preview of your video on the website's upload page.

UPLOADING 25%

Pick an eye-catching, clear **thumbnail** that will make people curious and want to see more.

| Farm | Pigs | Piglets | Chickens | Horses |
| Adventure | Exploring | Nature | Hay | Animals |

Adding **tags** helps people find your video when they search.

POST VIDEO

SHARE ON SOCIAL

Share the video on your own page or on pages covering similar topics.

Making an ident

An ident is the name given to the short animation or video clip that introduces a program, channel, or film. Creating an ident helps you introduce your video in around five to ten seconds. Use it to give yourself a familiar identity each time you upload a new video.

Purpose of an ident

There are many reasons why television, film, and online videos use idents. Here are some examples of idents. The best idents are always memorable. A viewer should be able to easily recall the look or concept behind an ident.

An ident creates an identity for the channel.

AUDITIONS ROUND 1
Next big thing
Subscribe 2.1 million

Creating your own

Your ident can be any style you like. It could be live-action, animation, or a mixture of the two. If you want to make an ident for a book review channel, think of some ideas that relate to reading. First brainstorm (map out) your ideas, and then choose one concept to bring to life.

Reveal name

Move each one

Stack of books

Book review

Flipping through pages

Time-lapse drawing

Brainstorming
Write down lots of ideas for your chosen ident.

Bringing it to life
You could move a stack of books to reveal your channel name.

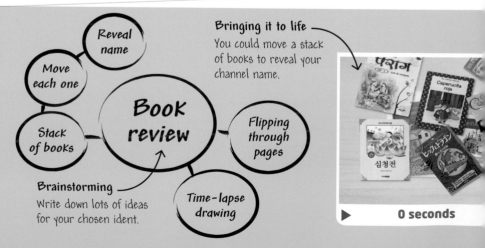

0 seconds

Words attract specific viewers

Little chef

Cooking show

Next big thing

Idents draw in the audience, increasing viewing figures.

762,804 Views

😊 73,802   😞 0

SCARY STORIES

Pictures and graphics add excitement.

Horror channel

2 seconds

4 seconds

Book Review Buddy

6 seconds

Glossary

actor/actress
Person who performs in a video

artificial
Something that is unnaturally produced

audience
People who watch a video or performance

audio
Sound that is recorded during filming

autofocus
Function that allows a camera to automatically focus the image

backdrop
Background that is behind a performer while they are being filmed

blooper
Funny mistake that is made during filming

brainstorm
When an individual or group comes up with new ideas

camera angle
Position a camera is in during filming

cast
Person or group of people who perform in a video

character
Person who is in a story

choreographer
Person who directs how the cast moves and dances

clapboard
Board that makes a sound when clapped together. It is used to sync audio with action

composer
Person who writes music for a video

crew
Person or group of people who work behind the scenes. They are involved in the production of a video

cue
Signal that tells an actor or actress to do something

cue card
Card that is held up to remind the cast what to do or say

dialogue
Words spoken by the actors and actresses during a performance

director
Person who tells the cast and crew what to do

drone
Remote-controlled flying machine that takes videos and pictures from above

editing
Process of putting pieces of footage together to make a complete video

end credits
Text shown at the end of a video listing everyone who helped make it

equipment
Items used to make a video, such as a camera, a tripod, and lighting

export
Turning a video into a file that can be shared online

exposure
Amount of light going into a camera

focus
Clearness of a picture or video

footage
Moving images that are recorded as files on a device

frame
Single, still shot that makes up part of a moving video

genre
Type or category of a video

gesture
Movement of the body that expresses a feeling

graphics
Visual images, often representing statistics or facts

green screen
Backdrop that can be digitally removed and replaced with something that was filmed separately

ident
Short animation or clip that introduces a program, channel, or film

import
Transferring footage from a camera or memory card to a computer or other device

lighting
Source of light for a scene, either natural (sunlight) or artificial (such as a lamp or a flashlight)

location
Place where the filming is done

memory card
Small card inside a camera that is used to store pictures and videos

microphone
Device that records sound

opening title
Clip shown at the start of a video listing the title and the people involved in making the video

pan
Moving the camera horizontally while filming

postproduction
Work done on a video after filming has happened

presenter
Person in a video who introduces it and usually talks throughout

process
Steps taken to complete a task

producer
Person who manages the making of a video

prop
Object that appears in a video

record
Capturing and saving moving images or sound

reflector
Surface that bounces light

rehearsal
Meeting to practice the script before a performance or a video shoot

review
Giving an opinion on something, which is often made public

scene
Series of shots taken in one location that makes up part of a video

script
Dialogue and directions for a performance

set
Scenery and props used to suggest a particular location

shoot
To capture images onto a camera

shot
Period when the camera is filming

smartphone
Cell phone that has similarities to a computer. It usually has a touchscreen, built-in camera, and Internet access

software
Program used by a computer

sound effects
Extra sounds added to a video when it is edited

speaker
Device that lets you hear sounds

special effects
Visual tricks that are handmade or digitally created for videos

stop-motion
Series of still images played together to give the illusion of motion

storyboard
Series of drawings that map out a plan for what will happen in a video

syncing
Matching up parts of a video so things happen at the same time

technique
Carrying out a task in a certain way

template
Guide to making something

time-lapse
Taking a video to capture slow changes and then speeding it up

tilt
Moving the camera vertically while filming

tracking
Moving and following the action with the camera

trailer
Short clips taken from a video to encourage people to watch it

transition
Changing from one shot to another

tripod
Three-legged stand that holds a camera steady

tutorial
Video that tells you how to do something

upload
To transfer a file from a computer to the Internet

viral
Video or image on the Internet that is viewed and passed on by many people

voice-over
Narration added to a video to explain information

zoom
Moving between wide and close-up shots

Index

Acknowledgments

The publisher would like to thank: Mohd Rizwan for image cut outs. Rashika Kachroo for managing image delivery. Allison Singer for additional illustration. Ewan Macdonald and Evan Raab for additional photography. Bella Grabham, our dog model on page 53.

The publisher would like to thank the following for their kind permission to reproduce their photographs (Key: a-above; b-below/bottom; c-center; f-far; l-left; r-right; t-top):

1 123RF.com: Damedeeso (bc). **4 123RF.com:** Aquira Phoyoo (bl); Gunnar Pippel / gunnar3000 (cl). **Alamy Stock Photo:** imageBROKER (br). **Dreamstime.com:** Eric Isselee (crb); Yongkiet (cl/ Camera view); Joserpizarro (cr). **5 123RF.com:** homy_design (t); Leung Cho Pan (l). **8 123RF.com:** snake3d (cr). **Alamy Stock Photo:** D. Hurst (cr). **Dorling Kindersley:** Lindsey Stock (cb); National Music Museum (c). **9 123RF.com:** belov1409 (cla). **Dreamstime.com:** Svetlana Yashina / Voinsveta (cb). **10 123RF.com:** Bonzami Emmanuelle (c); Ferli Achirulli (bc). **11 123RF.com:** Aquira Phoyoo (cb); dmbaker (cr); Gunnar Pippel / gunnar3000 (cr); Sataporn Jiwjalaen / Onairjiw (crb). **Dreamstime.com:** Dave Bredeson (tr); Yongkiet (c/ Camera view). **13 Alamy Stock Photo:** imageBROKER (cra). **14 Dreamstime.com:** Hotshotsworldwide (crb). **15 iStockphoto.com:** stockstudioX (b). **16 iStockphoto.com:** Jookimbkk (cb). **17 123RF.com:** Shaffandi (bc). **Alamy Stock Photo:** Anthony Brown (tl). **18 123RF.com:** Jillut (tr). **19 123RF.com:** Kanoksak Tameeraksa (cl); Paolo Airenti (cb). **Getty Images:** Jupiterimages (bl). **20 Getty Images:** Kathrin Ziegler (r, cb, bl). **21 Getty Images:** Kathrin Ziegler (cla, c, bl). **23 Dorling Kindersley:** Jemma Westing (cla). **Dreamstime.com:** Gow927 (cra). **24 Dorling Kindersley:** Gary Ombler (c). **Dreamstime.com:** Arenaphotouk (tc). **25 123RF.com:** Kostiantyn Kuznetsov (tc). **Alamy Stock Photo:** Bhandol (cra). **26 Getty Images:** Jupiterimages (bl). **26-27 123RF.com:** Dolgachov. **27 Alamy Stock Photo:** Angela Hampton Picture Library (bl). **28 Dreamstime.com:** Gow927 (cra). **Getty Images:** Jeffrey Penaloza / EyeEm (clb). **29 Dreamstime. com:** Anton Matushchak (br). **30-31 123RF.com:** Prapan Ngawkeaw. **34 Dreamstime.com:** Jacek Chabraszewski (r). **34-35 Dreamstime.com:** Nagy-bagoly Ilona (b). **35 123RF.com:** Ian Allenden (cla); luckybusiness (crb). **Dorling Kindersley:** Jemma Westing (bc). **36 Dreamstime. com:** Alexander Babich / Suricoma (crb); Sataporn Jiujalaen / Onairjiw (clb). **37 123RF.com:** Chris Brignell (cla); picsfive (ca); stokkete (cl). **Alamy Stock Photo:** Alexandre Zveiger (Background). **Dorling Kindersley:** Jemma Westing (cr).

Dreamstime.com: Alexei Novikov / Aruba2000 (cb); Sergey Sukhorukov / Acidgrey (cra). **38 123RF.com:** discovod (bl); Iakov Filimonov (bc). **40 123RF.com:** Sirichai Thaveesakvilai (cr). **Getty Images:** Peter Cade (br). **41 Alamy Stock Photo:** Christina Gandolfo (bc). **iStockphoto.com:** Ernie Decker (cr). **43 Dreamstime.com:** Torsak (cl). **44 iStockphoto.com:** skynesher (bl). **45 Dorling Kindersley:** Jemma Westing (crb). **Dreamstime. com:** Carlos Caetano (cr). **Getty Images:** Carol Yepes (cr/Astronaut). **48 Dreamstime.com:** Andersastphoto (cra). **48-49 Dreamstime.com:** Photographerlondon. **49 123RF.com:** Christian Musat (cb). **Dreamstime.com:** Luis Louro (fcrb); Mozzyb (crb); Toniflap (fcrb/Andes). **50 Ewan Macdonald:** (br). **51 123RF.com:** Maglara (t). **Alamy Stock Photo:** Mark Green (t/Dinosaur). **Getty Images:** Dirk Anschutz (bl). **52 123RF.com:** anyka (cra); Kirill Kedrinski (cr); Jaromir Chalabala (crb). **Dreamstime.com:** Colorburst (bl). **52-53 Alamy Stock Photo:** Christina Gandolfo (b). **56 123RF.com:** gstockstudio (cb); Vitalii Tiahunov (c, crb); Mile Atanasov (c/Fitness tracker); wstockstudio (cl). **Dreamstime.com:** Alexroz (crb/ Watch); Axstokes (cb/Phone); Michael Flippo (b); Julien Tromeur (br). **Getty Images:** Richard Boll (cr). **58 Ala Uddin:** (r). **60 123RF.com:** Varin Rattanaburi (br). **Alamy Stock Photo:** Clement Morin (tr). **iStockphoto.com:** AleksandarNakic (cb). **60-61 iStockphoto.com:** AleksandarNakic. **61**

Evan Raab: (b). **62 123RF.com:** Maglara (bl). **63 123RF.com:** Bidouze Stephane (crb); Otnaydur (cla); My Visuals (cb). **Getty Images:** Peter Cade (cra). **64 Dreamstime.com:** Christoph Weihs / Aeolos (cr). **65 Alamy Stock Photo:** Hero Images Inc. (crb, fcrb). **Dreamstime.com:** Andersastphoto (crb/Computer). **Getty Images:** Digital Vision / Thomas Northcut (clb). **66-67 Dreamstime.com:** Christoph Weihs / Aeolos (c). **67 123RF.com:** Sergey Ma-Yu-Kun / maukun (ca). **Dreamstime. com:** Christoph Weihs / Aeolos (crb); Paulwongkwan / Kwan Wong (cb). **iStockphoto. com:** tortoon (crb/Wood). **69 123RF.com:** Nejron (bl, bc/Girl, br, fbr). **Dreamstime.com:** Dmitry Islentyev (cr). **70 Alamy Stock Photo:** Hero Images Inc. (bc, br); Terry Harris (cra); imageBROKER (crb). **Dreamstime.com:** Melvinlee (cb). **71 123RF.com:** creativemarc (ca/Park). **Alamy Stock Photo:** Antonio Guillem Fernández (ca/Girl, ca/Girl 1); Terry Harris (cla); Hero Images Inc. (crb, fcrb). **Dreamstime.com:** Andersastphoto (br); Stanko Mravljak / Stana (cla/Snow, ca). **75 Dreamstime.com:** Orangesquid (cb). **76-77 Getty Images:** Digital Vision / Thomas Northcut (ca). **77 Dreamstime.com:** Christoph Weihs / Aeolos (cb)

All other images © Dorling Kindersley
For further information see: www.dkimages.com